Dad was cross.

Dad was sad.

Kevin had been very bad.

Lotty was cross.

Lotty was mad.

Kevin had been very bad.

A leg of ham was on a tray.

Kevin took the ham away.

Then he hid it from
his dad.
Kevin had been very
bad.

'Look,' said Dad. 'The ham has gone.
Is this something you have done?'

Kevin was red.

Kevin was sad.

'Yes. I hid it,' he said to Dad.

So Kevin went to get the ham.

'I am sorry. I really am.'

‘You and Lotty eat it up.

I have been a silly pup.’